How the Birds Stop Singing
Stories of Drug and Alcohol Abuse as Told to a Doctor

by
Jamilé Wakim Fleming MD

with
Oriana Marie
Donna M. Lauer

This book is dedicated to our families

ACKNOWLEDGMENTS

For their help in completing this project, we would like to thank Joelle E. Fleming, Seong-Ae Mun and Robert Sberna. And a special thank you to all who shared their stories with us.

TABLE OF CONTENTS

PREFACE

Recent drug overdose statistics are shocking. Northeast Ohio, where I live, is on pace to record more than 500 overdose deaths this year from heroin. Most of them are teenagers.

In just one day in Sept. 2016, seven teens in the Cleveland area died of a drug overdose. They left behind grieving families and friends.

As a medical professional and parent, I am deeply concerned that drug abuse is destroying the lives of so many young people and fracturing their families and communities.

While growing up in war-torn Lebanon, running from bombings and certain death was a way of life for us. But now, it is heartbreaking for me to watch so many teenagers willingly putting their lives in danger by using deadly drugs.

In my medical practice, I've seen firsthand the devastating effects of drugs and alcohol. After hearing so many young patients tell me they didn't know the seriousness of drug abuse, I decided to take steps to impact this situation and perhaps help save the lives of even a few young people. With this book, I hope to share the reality and consequences of substance abuse.

Along with my co-authors, I went searching for answers directly from people who have survived drug addiction. Speaking candidly of their experiences, these survivors can have a deep influence in changing the minds of those tempted by addicting substances.

This book is about prevention. It is targeted towards young people who may be at risk of using addicting drugs and alcohol.

We explain how toxic substances, whether legal or

not, can damage the body and cause untimely death. We also highlight how important it is to know what—and how much—of these substances we put in our bodies. Because although we may have a second chance to survive when severely intoxicated with alcohol, it's very possible that we may not survive the first use of drugs.

Jamilé Wakim Fleming
Sept. 2016

There is no telling what tune they would have sung if they had survived. And no telling what effect their song would have had on a lonely soul, a broken heart or an ailing body. Young and fearless, they chose a path where there is no singing.

Only those who have survived can know.

1. High Tolerance

Dee was 20 years old when I first met her at a college fair. Just as we began our conversation, she received a shocking phone call. When she ended the call, there were tears rolling from her eyes. Speaking to me between sobs, she said, "My cousin just died in a car accident. I can't believe it, we were going to meet later today for dinner."

Tearfully, she recounted stories about her cousin while we stood next to each other half-frozen in the aftershock of the sad news. Dee's cousin, a young man, had died while under the influence of alcohol.

"I drink too," she told me. "I joined a sorority in college. We used to drink a lot but I have a high tolerance to alcohol; my cousin didn't have any tolerance to it. He got drunk quickly and often. He couldn't handle alcohol like I do and that's what killed him."

Dee, like many other young people, believes that having a high tolerance to alcohol is a good thing. But in fact it is a very bad thing. Here's how: When we drink for the first time, we usually feel sleepy or drunk—depending on the amount and the type of alcohol ingested. The next time, the same amount of alcohol may not cause any problems, leaving us to feel safe to drink more. We think we can tolerate larger amounts each time we drink, so we keep on drinking. Sometimes, however, the alcohol can reach a toxic level in our body and kills us.

The National Institutes of Health (NIH) defines tolerance as a state in which an organism no longer responds to a drug and a higher dose is required to achieve the same effect.

Drinking alcohol in moderation is not bad for healthy people. In fact up to 2 drinks a night is not going to send a healthy person to the hospital. But some people may be more sensitive to alcohol than others.

" Dee," I implored, "before you crack open that bottle of wine, you should know that it's possible to drink the same amount as some of your friends and end up the only one with serious problems." Dee lifted one eyebrow and stared at me without saying a word.

Usually, mental status is the first to be affected by alcohol, but the changes may be subtle and not clearly evident to individuals who drink too much. These changes range from difficulty with sleeping, driving a car, or keeping up good grades. These nuances in behavior indicate that damage to the brain has already begun. If people continue to drink, then gradually alcohol becomes more and more toxic and their entire body will suffer until they fall very ill. Many 20- and 30-year-old people are admitted to the hospital in serious condition as a result of alcohol intoxication and some of them end up dying.

"At age 20? From alcohol?" she exclaimed.

"Even though young people may think they can drink without a problem, drinking to excess causes blood alcohol levels to reach a point at which their body will eventually collapse.

"High tolerance can actually be detrimental to your health. Keep this in mind, and evaluate the amount of alcohol you consume. It might be time to cut back." I emphasized.

2. Alcohol and the Body

"How exactly does alcohol damage the body?" Dee asked me.

"Alcohol hurts the body in many ways," I replied. "And some of these ways go unnoticed because we are not always able to accurately measure alcohol toxicity, which is unfortunate to the people who drink."

Dee looked at me with big curious eyes eager to understand what I was telling her. "When ingested," I continued, "alcohol goes from the stomach to the intestines where it gets absorbed in the blood and carried all the way to the liver. The liver is like a factory that filters the blood and sorts out the good stuff from the bad stuff. By doing so, it removes the toxins from the blood to cleanse it before it reaches the rest of the body. But when alcohol is ingested in large amounts, the liver becomes overwhelmed and won't be able to keep up with the detoxification process. It fills up with toxic products from alcohol and from inflammation, and becomes large and tender. People may feel sick like they have the flu or they may think they have a stomach bug. Because they feel sick, they may end up drinking more alcohol to try to feel better, which causes more damage to their liver until it shuts down. The liver normally filters out bilirubin (a substance that turns people yellow), but a damaged liver can't remove bilirubin, so it collects and causes jaundice (yellowness) to appear in the skin and in the eyes.

"It is important," I continued, "to read the labels on alcohol bottles, because alcohol toxicity depends on the amount and the concentration of what you're drinking. For example a standard drink in the U.S. is about 14 grams of pure alcohol. That's one can of beer, one glass of wine, or one shot of hard liquor (rum, vodka or whiskey). The more concentrated the alcohol, the less of it you can drink before your liver becomes overwhelmed. Usually alcohol becomes toxic when people have ingested 80 grams of pure alcohol, which is very easy to reach."

"Wow," Dee leaned back in her chair. "That's only six cans of beer. My friends and I often drink more than that in a night."

I nodded. "It gets worse. Even though there is a general threshold beyond which toxicity from alcohol is more likely, every person responds to alcohol differently because of their genetic make-up, their gender, their weight, and their metabolism."

Then I pleaded: "Dee, it's important to remember that not everyone reacts to alcohol the same way. Try to understand how your body reacts to alcohol and what amount of alcohol is likely to affect your personality, your behavior and your normal functioning, and try not to exceed that amount."

Dee scoffed. "So you're saying never drink or get drunk? Sorry to tell you, Doc, but that's not going to happen."

"That's your choice, but I just want you to know what you're getting into," I replied. "Be prepared. Keep track of drinks and ask friends and family to cut you off, to avoid excessive drinking."

I explained to Dee that women are more sensitive to alcohol than men and therefore prone to more toxicity if they drink the same amount as men do. Dee, like many others, was not aware of this. She told me that when she goes to parties with her friends they drink as much as the guys. Although it's often a point of pride to match 'the guys' drink for drink, it is very dangerous for many reasons. First, women are generally smaller than men and alcohol filters out slower in their bodies. Secondly, they have more body fat which can store larger amounts of alcohol. And thirdly, women lack the stomach enzymes that men have. These enzymes break down the alcohol and make it less toxic before it gets in the blood. This basically means that women do not tolerate alcohol like men do and they will have more symptoms like nausea, vomiting, diarrhea or bleeding, even if they do not get drunk.

"Yeah, I've gotten sick like that." Dee mumbled quietly. Then her voice suddenly perked up and she declared, " But I heard coffee is good for your liver, how about drinking more coffee to protect the liver from alcohol?"

"But the story isn't over yet!" I answered. "There are more situations that affect our toxicity to alcohol. For example, coffee does seem to have some protective effects on the liver—but it's not protective enough. All the coffee in the world can't reverse the effects of too much alcohol. Also, drinking without food is more harmful than drinking with meals, and it is common for people who drink to skip meals altogether. Missing meals depletes the body of nutrients and vitamins necessary for the detoxification process of alcohol. Drinking while taking certain medications is another situation that makes alcohol more toxic and it's very important to avoid taking drugs like acetaminophen also known as Tylenol while drinking. This combination of alcohol and Tylenol can kill—and has killed—even the healthiest people."

As we continued our discussion, Dee kept talking about beer as if beer is not real alcohol. Like Dee, many people believe that beer is less harmful than other types of alcohol so they feel safe to drink a lot. Some people believe that beer and wine are not alcohol. While it is true that beer is less potent than rum or vodka, alcohol is alcohol! A 12-ounce can of beer is the equivalent of 5 ounces of wine or 1.5 ounces of liquor. All are alcohol, all are potentially harmful.

"Well…I kind of knew that doctor," Dee admitted.

I then told her that individuals addicted to alcohol will turn to nearly any substance if they are craving a buzz. For example, hospital emergency rooms see many people who have unintentionally poisoned themselves by drinking cleaning products from their own house.

Numerous household items contain alcohol, making them an easy choice for people with addiction problems. Whether feeding their addiction or avoiding withdrawal symptoms, people with addictions sometimes turn to toxic household products when they run out of money. This behavior often leads to death because household items are extremely toxic. Swallowing these substances destroys the lining of the swallowing tube (also called esophagus), the stomach, and possibly other internal organs. They cause ulcers that bleed and serious problems later in life if the person survives. These products not only contain alcohol, but they also contain toxic ingredients in high concentrations and that's a double whammy.

Dee was starting to understand how the liver functions and how toxic alcohol can be. Then she said, "But I've heard that red wine is supposed to be good for you. Most every person in the world drinks wine! They can't be all stupid!"

"Wine is good to a certain degree," I replied. "But the general concept that alcohol is good for you is false. Small amounts of alcohol can lower the bad cholesterol level, which may protect you from heart attacks and strokes. But the cons outweigh the pros and it's easy to get carried away and drink to excess. This puts people at risk for addiction, alcoholism and serious injuries. Preteens and teen-agers are the most vulnerable group for toxicity because their organs are not fully developed yet and when they drink, they are most likely to become alcoholics and to combine alcohol with many other drugs. These combinations can be—and usually are—

lethal."

Alcohol can damage the brain, the heart, the liver, the muscles and the pancreas. It also increases the risk of cancer of the liver, mouth, throat, larynx and esophagus. It can cause high blood pressure and psychological problems. It weakens the immune system and puts people at risk for infections. In pregnant women, alcohol causes fetal alcohol syndrome: Their babies will have brain damage, growing problems, poor mental and motor skills and low IQ. As they grow up, these children are sometimes prone to committing criminal activities.

In addition to harming themselves, people who drink may endanger others. Driving under the influence of alcohol is often a factor in fatal car accidents. According to the Centers for Disease Control and Prevention (CDC), at least 10,000 people are killed per year in alcohol-related crashes. That is one-third of all traffic deaths in the United States!

"Think of it this way," I said, "deaths due to drugs and alcohol are not caused by natural diseases, these deaths are self-inflicted and so easily preventable!"

Laws have been passed to minimize and prevent alcohol-related crashes. And in most states, the blood alcohol concentration level (BAC) for driving is set to be less than 0.08 percent, but levels of BAC as low as 0.02 percent have caused problems with mood and sleep, vision and ability to multi-task, as well as performance in school.

"Oh my gosh, 0.02 percent seems very low."

"Yes. So it is always good to know the limit and the dangers of drinking," I emphasized.

"I have a friend, Mary. She is on her way to join us," Dee said. "Mary only drinks once a week on Saturdays, but she sometimes drinks two bottles of wine. Her dad died from alcoholism. She didn't want to end up like him so she doesn't drink every day like he did. But based on what you told me the other day, I kind of explained to her that she is drinking too much, am I correct?"

Before I could respond, Mary walked in the door. She had a big smile and wore a large navy blue scarf wrapped around her neck and shoulders. I found myself noticing her stylish attire. Layers of silver chains covered the front of her scarf. Her nose and earlobes were pierced in three places, and shimmery earrings peeked out between the strands of her long hair.

"I don't even come close to drinking as much as my father did," she said emphatically. "He used to drink a lot every day. I only drink once a week. I usually get drunk, but then I stop the rest of the week to give my body some rest."

I waited for her to finish, then I told her, "This is called binge drinking. And I need to tell you that it is as bad as drinking excessively."

Mary's eyes widened and I could tell I had her full attention. "Binge drinking," I explained, "is when someone drinks a lot quickly—as much as 5 or more drinks on a single occasion for men, or 4 or more drinks on a single occasion for women."

By these standards, Mary was binge drinking and abusing alcohol. Alcohol abuse is a pattern of drinking that harms one's health, their interpersonal relationships, and their ability to work. Over time, this leads to alcohol dependence and addiction. People with alcohol addiction continue to drink despite repeated physical, psychological, or interpersonal problems, and they are unable to limit their drinking.

"It makes no difference to me what it's called, I don't drink every day, and people can recover if they stop for awhile. That's what I've heard. Am I not correct?" Mary asked, somewhat defiantly.

"But sometimes the damage is not reversible and there is no going back," I replied. "That's why the CDC posted consumption guidelines for people. In fact, some people should not drink alcoholic beverages at all. These people are children and adolescents, women who may become pregnant or who are pregnant, individuals who plan to drive, operate machinery, or take part in activities that require attention and coordination, individuals taking prescription or over-the-counter medications that can interact with alcohol, individuals with medical problems, and persons recovering from alcoholism."

"Okay, but how does alcohol continue to hurt the body when people stop drinking?" Dee asked. "I always thought that if you give your liver a break, it will recover quickly."

"Sometimes when people drink regularly and for many years, the damage to the liver is too far advanced and the liver becomes inflamed and cirrhotic. When the drinking stops, the inflammation in the liver may improve and the liver can gain some of its normal functions. But the cirrhosis may not improve. In most cases, there is no way to know for sure if the liver will recover until some time has passed with absolutely no alcohol. Without alcohol there is usually a good chance for some recovery. So it's never too late to stop drinking! But if a person doesn't stop, they will inevitably suffer from liver failure and die unless the diseased liver is replaced with a new liver as in liver transplantation. But the problem with liver transplantation is finding a donor in a timely manner to replace the bad liver before the person dies. Since not a lot of people are donating organs to meet the demands, people who need a liver end up dying while waiting for a new liver."

"That's sad," Dee said, adding in a soft voice that she is a registered organ donor.

"What is also very sad," I added, "is that young people are dying from alcohol toxicity even before they have cirrhosis."

I explained that alcohol toxicity can happen in young people when they drink too much in a very short time, even before they get drunk or have cirrhosis. This is also called acute alcoholic hepatitis. It is a very dangerous situation because the liver becomes severely inflamed and shuts down quickly causing other organs to shut down too. In this situation people are at a very high risk of dying.

"But doesn't the liver regenerate itself?"

"This is another misconception," I said. "A diseased liver with cirrhosis does not regenerate a healthy liver. It needs to be replaced as is done in liver transplantation. Whereas a healthy liver will regenerate a healthy liver and will grow back to its original size if a piece of it is removed, as is done in live liver donation. In live donation, a healthy person donates part of their liver to someone else to replace their diseased liver."

Normally, the liver prevents infections and removes bacteria from the blood. It helps regulate the blood sugar, makes proteins that help build muscle, and produces substances that help the blood clot when there is bleeding. It also stores vitamins and nutrients and excretes bile to get rid of excess bilirubin and other toxins. All these functions are lost when the liver is overwhelmed by alcohol.

The pancreas is another organ that can be destroyed by alcohol. People will suffer with severe pain for many years before they die of pancreatitis. They end up taking too many pain killers which over time cause addiction and drug abuse. Pancreatitis may cause premature death and cancer of the pancreas.

Alcohol can also ruin the nervous system. It damages the brain and also damages the nerves. When this happens, people end up with memory loss, poor gait and coordination, and tingling and numbness in their hands and feet. It is common for alcoholics to become deficient

in vitamins like vitamin B for example, that are necessary for the normal functioning of the nervous system.
Without these vitamins, people end up with dementia and conditions known as Wernicke-Korsakof encephalopathy which can be very serious.

The heart is another organ that can be damaged by excessive drinking. Too much drinking causes the heart muscle to weaken and dilate. The heart then expands like a balloon and it won't be able to pump the blood out to the rest of the body. This condition is called heart failure and it kills.

The kidneys also suffer from excessive alcohol. People may end up on dialysis because of kidney failure. In dialysis the blood is run through a machine outside the body 3 times a week for about 4 hours each time. The machine will do the job of the kidneys to clean the blood otherwise the person dies. Dialysis is associated with many complications and will make it difficult for people to have a normal life. Sometimes they get a kidney transplantation if a donor kidney becomes available.

Our body is not impermeable. We are constantly absorbing stuff—food when we eat and air when we breathe. We absorb directly from the skin, the nose and from the lining inside our mouth and our intestines, and from the lungs. The things we absorb enter the blood and are carried to our organs. Normally we absorb good things that help our body to stay alive, but in alcoholics (and drug users), the body allows toxins, bacteria, viruses and fungi to invade our organs and cause infections.

"Normally," I said, "the healthy body has all the tools to fight these germs and keep them in control. When the body fails, our cells are unable to perform their usual functions. Germs become free to circulate and take up nutrients and vitamins from the body to feed themselves and to reproduce, until a total germ invasion has taken place. We call this sepsis. Sepsis kills at least one million people every year in the U.S. and alcoholics and drug users are specifically prone to sepsis."

"I can see how alcohol can be so bad for us" Dee said.

"Yeah," said Mary, "but these are extreme situations. I will stop drinking way before any of this will ever happen to me."

"I hope you do," I added. "But sometimes it is very difficult to stop on your own. You should not hesitate to ask for help from a doctor who may be able to prescribe medications that help you break the addiction, and from a rehab counselor who will help you stay away from alcohol and drugs. But none of this will help if you are not serious about quitting. And the sooner you seek help, the more likely you are to succeed at quitting and overcoming your addiction."

3. Addicting Drugs and Narcan

One morning, Dee called me: "Did you hear the news? It's all over Facebook. A bunch of kids died last night of heroin use. This seems to be happening more often. It's crazy. What is going on?"

"Yes, I'm aware of a spike in deaths," I told her. Then I began to explain the dangers of heroin. It's a powerful opioid that produces euphoria and feelings of relaxation and pleasure. Just one dose can cause a person to stop breathing and die. If a person does not die immediately, he or she will develop symptoms of toxicity like a dry mouth, skin discoloration, small pupils and a drop in blood pressure."

Dee interjected: " I bet most heroin addicts know these symptoms."

" You may be right." I added. And there are more problems with heroin. After the drop in blood pressure, the body becomes stiff and the person falls into coma and dies. When smoked, heroin causes severe lung damage and emphysema which is an extremely slow process of suffocation. It may take many years of slow suffocation before people die, and that is very debilitating. When injected into the veins, heroin can cause serious infections."

Like most drugs bought on the street, heroin is often mixed with other toxins which makes it even more dangerous. Heroin use causes 90 percent of deaths related to illegal substance use. Increasingly, we've seen that heroin is mixed with fentanyl, a synthetic opioid that is similar to morphine, but 50 to 100 times more potent. The combination of heroin and fentanyl has led to skyrocketing death rates.

Of course, illegal and toxic drugs sold on the street are not regulated by U.S. pharmacies or the Food and Drug

Administration (FDA), so no one knows what their exact composition is. Because of their varying potency, one dose may be more than enough to kill a person.

"Dee," I said, "you need to be aware that drugs sold on the streets are mixed with more dangerous substances that makes them extremely risky, and that's what is happening these days."

After I explained the dangers of heroin, Dee wanted to hear about other drugs and specifically about marijuana (cannabis). She called Mary over to join us the next morning.

"Marijuana is legal now," Dee said.

"Yes and the most commonly used substance worldwide," I replied.

According to the CDC, there are over 160 million marijuana users in the US and 2.4 million new users every year, and these numbers are rising. But there are dangers involved in using marijuana. When ingested by pregnant women, marijuana crosses the placenta and affects the fetus. If the fetus is intoxicated, it won't grow normally, ending up with malformations and defects in the brain and the rest of the body.

Marijuana enters breast milk as well, and can cause the breast-feeding baby to be sick and to grow up with problems with memory, learning ability, attention focus, coordination and reaction time. People who use marijuana are not able to drive vehicles safely because their reaction time is slowed significantly. In addition, cannabis increases heart rate or pulse and can cause kidney problems, lung problems and mental or psychological problems. People become psychotic and they hallucinate. Some studies suggest that heavy cannabis use in the teen years is associated with declines in IQ scores later in life. Several states have allowed the use of marijuana for medicinal purposes to treat seizures, headaches, and the side effects caused by chemotherapy in people with cancer. Like any other substance however, it is not without problems especially if used for long periods.

Reports in *Science Magazine* found that even when used for medical purposes, marijuana may not be as effective as proclaimed to be. *The Journal of the American Medical Association* reports that marijuana increases dizziness, dry mouth, nausea, fatigue, sleepiness, loss of balance and hallucinations. Many other symptoms like acute intoxications, dependence and withdrawal symptoms have also been reported with marijuana use. Marijuana is available in various forms like leaves, hash, oil, and wax.

Like all drugs, the side effects of marijuana depend on its purity, its contents, and its concentration. Since these varieties are not regulated by the FDA, their use can be extremely dangerous and reports on marijuana's toxicity are on the rise since its legalization and widespread use. Synthetic cannabinoids (marijuana created in chemistry labs) can be more dangerous than the natural cannabinoids that grow as a plant. In states that have legalized synthetic cannabinoids, a sharp increase in emergency room visits have been reported because of heart attacks, seizures, difficulty walking, coma and death. Some people use "K2" or "Spice" instead of marijuana, but it is highly addictive and produces the same symptoms as marijuana. It is used almost as frequently as marijuana by high school students.

And so we kept on discussing more drugs, one after the other.

Cocaine is a short-acting stimulant and can lead users to "binge" in a single session. Cocaine use has caused severe problems with the heart, the lungs, the nervous and the digestive systems. Cocaine users can experience severe paranoia, in which they lose touch with reality. Their behavior becomes dangerous and they may commit crimes. The powdered form of cocaine is either inhaled through the nose (snorted), or dissolved in water and injected via a needle into the blood. Crack or freebase cocaine is a form of cocaine that has been processed to make a rock crystal. It is usually smoked and when heated, its vapors get into the blood through the lungs and cause problems.

MDMA (Ecstasy or "Molly") and LSD are common hallucinogens. They cause mind-altering and stimulant effects. Users see vivid colors and images, hear sounds and feel sensations that seem real but do not exist. These changes cause the person to perform dangerous behaviors and commit crimes. They also increase body temperature, heart rate, blood pressure, and toxicity to the nerves. LSD is the most potent hallucinogen, coming in different forms such as liquid, capsule or painted on papers that can be licked.

PCP was developed in the 1950s as an anesthetic for patients undergoing surgery. It was discontinued 10 years later because it caused serious problems and many deaths. Unfortunately, PCP is still sold on the street and its use outside medical supervision is super dangerous. PCP is usually sprayed on leafy vegetables and ingested, but it can also be taken as a pill or injected in liquid form into veins. PCP causes brain problems like hallucinations, seizures, coma and death.

Ketamine, a derivative of PCP, Gamma hydroxybutyrate (GHB), and Rohypnol benzodiazepines are agents that cause depression of the nervous system, which causes excessive sleepiness and loss of consciousness. They are known as date rape drugs because they also cause memory loss. They can easily be added to beverages and ingested unknowingly, which makes it possible for sexual abuse to occur.

Inhalants are volatile substances that people inhale or breathe. This way, inhalants go directly to the lungs.

Some common inhalants are glue, shoe polish, spray paints, gasoline, and lighter fluid. Other inhalants are found in many household products such as oven cleaners, gasoline, spray paints, and other aerosols. They are extremely toxic and can damage the heart, the kidneys, the lungs, and the brain. It is a common misconception that inhalants are safe because they are inhaled and not injected. This is false because we absorb what we inhale in our lungs, which gets absorbed into the blood and the rest of the body. Even healthy people can suffer a heart attack and die within minutes of using an inhalant for the first time.

Nicotine is an addictive stimulant found in cigarettes and other forms of tobacco. According to the World Health Organization's Report on Global Tobacco Epidemics released in 2008, tobacco smoke increases the risk of various cancers, breathing and heart problems. Firsthand users aren't the only ones affected; secondhand inhalers who do not smoke are also at risk for cancers and for heart problems. Although smoking rates have decreased in the U.S., the mortality rate is still staggering with more than 480,000 deaths happening each year.

Pure caffeine powder is another toxic substance. The FDA is warning about its use and toxicity. Pure caffeine powder is about 30 times more potent than the amount of caffeine in a regular cup of coffee, which makes it very dangerous. Like other toxic products purchasable in the streets, the pure caffeine powder has been mixed with other toxins, increasing its deadliness. Caffeine powder is a stimulant, causing several symptoms ranging from vomiting and diarrhea to dangerously irregular heartbeat, seizures, coma and death.

Some medications are approved by the FDA under defined schedules based on their level of toxicity, but they are regularly abused. Examples of these are opioid pain killers (morphine, OxyContin, Vicodin, and

Percodan), stimulants (cocaine, ecstasy, MDMA, caffeine and nicotine), and depressants (benzodiazepines and barbiturates). Because they are used medically and prescribed by physicians, there is a belief that they are safe. Use of these drugs without medical prescriptions is extremely dangerous and to make matters worse, these substances are often taken in combination with alcohol and other drugs, making them even more dangerous.

Approximately one out of 35 people between the ages of 12-18 are using illegal drugs based on the CDC reports in 2013. This means that in every classroom in grade school there was an average of one student using an illegal substance. These numbers are rising. Fatal doses of heroin have reached a record high in 2015 and they are expected to reach another record in 2016. What is making the fight on drugs difficult is that as soon as laws take effect making a substance illegal, manufacturers of these drugs come up with new chemicals that are more toxic than the prior generation of drugs, and they label them with new names outdating these laws almost immediately.

"It's almost impossible to ban every single dangerous substance, so it's up to you to stay aware, and avoid them! There may not be a second chance to survive when using drugs, and people often die before they have the chance to make it to the hospital." I emphasized

"But I heard they came up with a new drug that saves lives," Mary stated with a reassuring tone.

"Yes, you're talking about Narcan," I concurred.

Narcan also known as Naloxone, Nalone or Evzio is an FDA-approved drug that is given when someone using heroin is intoxicated. Police officers began using it in the U.S. in 2014 to save the lives of those who have overdosed. The American Medical Association endorses the training of non-medical professionals such as family, friends and whoever is interested, including drug users, in recognizing signs of toxicity from opioids and in the administration of Narcan. It is becoming readily available outside medical clinics, and people using drugs should know that Narcan saves lives if given promptly. However several doses may need to be given. When other toxins are mixed in with heroin, Narcan may not be very effective because it is never clear what the other toxins are. Narcan comes in an easy to administer nasal spray and is generally safe to use without side effects when given to the person who is intoxicated. However, Narcan does not prevent addictive behavior and even if Narcan is given, an emergency medical team should be called and the intoxicated individual should be admitted to the hospital when released from the emergency room, or taken to a rehab center in order to begin rehab very promptly.

In addition to toxicity from the drugs used, when people snort or inject drugs, they often share straws and needles or re-use them again non-sterilized. By doing so they are introducing germs like bacteria and viruses from the dirty needles directly into their blood and from there to the rest of the body. These germs cause serious infections and can kill a person. Bacteria and viruses like HIV; viral hepatitis B, C, D; and other viruses have caused large epidemics and killed millions of people in the US and worldwide. Vaccines to prevent viruses are effective in protecting those who receive them, but there are no vaccines for all the viruses, and medications are not always curative.

"Doc, people want to try everything even if they know it is bad," Mary said. "But, as you said, if they are informed and know what they are getting themselves into, maybe they won't start."

I nodded in agreement, then said, "At least, they should not share dirty needles or straws with anyone else, and not even reuse their own dirty needles. They should get vaccinated and carry Narcan and condoms, and not be afraid to dial 911 if someone overdoses. These are life-saving tools."

4. In Their Own Words

CJ started using heroin at age 40. One day she woke up not feeling well. Her partner gave her a sniff of heroin to try and she immediately felt better. "Everything in my body felt good so I used it again and again until I got hooked. Then I started shooting in my veins and I ended up with an infection in my heart from reusing my own dirty needle. I almost died," she said.

CJ used to buy heroin and cocaine and mix them with talc and other powders to triple their size. She would then sell them on the street for at least 3 times the price she bought them for in order to make a living selling drugs.

"But people have died from the drugs you sold!" I exclaimed

"Yes they have, but I was not trying to kill them," she countered. "I wanted money and they wanted to get high. These drugs are all over the place. If somebody wants to get high, they will go to any lengths. I've known people who drank shoe polish to feed their addiction. They will get drugs anywhere if not from me. This stuff makes them feel good."

"But they know drugs are harmful," I said. "Why do you think people want to hurt themselves?"

"It's not intentional. For example, I was raised in a strict religious home. We went to church on Sunday and bible school afterwards. We were trained to be moral and good. Then I met this man who became my fiancé and I was going to marry him."

"How old were you?"

"18. He was 5 years older and had a job in a different state. I thought he was the man for me and I was ready to grow up and be independent. But I was young and in a new place. I didn't know anyone and I wanted to please him. I had become dependent on him. I had no personality. All I cared about was making him happy. He fell in love with someone else and left me. My world was shattered. Things got very bad for me and I began using drugs and ended up on the street. I had no other place to go. To get drugs, I exchanged sex for money."

"What finally brought you home?"

"My mother went looking for me. When I saw her I remembered how life was back home. Now, I am off drugs and beginning college."

"You were lucky."

"Yes," she said. "My mother found me before I overdosed and died."

"How many of your friends died using drugs?"

"I saw a handful die in front of me. It was the worst experience of my life."

Fay did not start shooting drugs until she was in her 30s.

"How did you begin?"

"I was doing well until I got married. I had 3 kids. I was constantly tired and wanted some way to be happy and break the daily routine."

"Were children and family life overwhelming?"

"My husband was away all the time, having affairs and doing illegal things. I needed his presence so bad. He started using me to pose for webcam modeling jobs and getting me into all sorts of illegal things to make money. He later became physically abusive. He beat me badly."

"Did you tell your parents?"

"No. I was embarrassed about the things I did. I was embarrassed to tell them. I knew what I was doing was wrong but I felt trapped and ashamed."

"When you started using drugs, your kids were young. Didn't he care?"

"I was 15 when I had my first child and my youngest was a newborn when I started doing drugs. He did not care."

"And then what happened?"

"I ended up in jail. In retrospect, it was the best thing that could have happened to me. They sent me to rehab afterwards. When I look back now at what I did, I don't believe it." She started crying. "I lost custody of my kids. It is not worth it"

5. Peer Influence

"Peer influence can be a life saver: They helped you start; together you can stop."

There are many reasons why people begin using drugs. Some do it to get out of a difficult time in their life, others say they want to defy their parents. But most of the time it is peer influence. You may run away from peer pressure but you may not run away from peer influence because it is a simple request from another user asking you to try just once. That is why I call it peer influence and it is powerful enough to get you hooked. In the grip of peer influence, you trust the people who offer you drugs at a weak moment in your life and since they are not pressuring you, you feel you can trust them. You may refuse once or twice but they will eventually get you when you are bored, stressed, or feeling tired and sick. They've made you curious to try by simply suggesting it and you try the first time. "Only once," you convince yourself because you want to find out if the drug will truly make you feel better. This is your fatal move!

Lauren was 20 when I spoke to her. She had used heroin since she was 17 years old and never had real problems with it. She asked me, "Is it really that bad, will all these problems really happen?"

Lauren hadn't died from heroin, so she believed that everything was going to be okay—it couldn't kill her. She survived every time she used it but she knew that heroin was very addicting and she relapsed many times after she thought she had stopped.

"I hated the pain of withdrawal and I wanted more drugs," she said. She told me she got her first dose from her boyfriend. "I did not realize I liked opiates so much. When I went through withdrawal, I hated the *dopesick* feeling and I was always looking for something to make me feel better and feed my addiction. I got pregnant then I had a miscarriage which threw me into depression and I went back to using heroin again."

"Have you ever been in jail?"

"Yes. But every time life got difficult, I would go back to drugs. It was easier than dealing with people and trying to fix things, I wanted to feel better instantly and nothing will do it like drugs."

"When was the last time you used?"

"A month ago." She paused, then said, "I will never go back to it."

"How are you sure this time?"

"Eventually, I came to not like the way it makes me feel, I've been getting sick lately and going from one emergency room to the other."

I stayed in contact with Lauren, who returned to heroin. This time she wasn't so lucky. She was taken to the emergency room one day and stayed in a drug-induced coma until she died.

DJ was bullied and was afraid to go to school until he found some friends. They were all on drugs but at least he had friends now.

"Drugs killed loneliness at school," he said. "If your friends do it, you will do it too."

A few decades ago, 20-year-olds were getting married and knew what their future would be. Nowadays, jobs are scarce and unpredictable, and life is tougher. In addition, drugs are readily accessible and it takes much more effort to avoid their temptations.

DJ is sober now. He reflected: "Every action begins with a thought. Knowing your body and having a back-up plan to protect your body will save your life. Kids using drugs know which drugs are the most addicting based on their personal experience. They advise each other to avoid heroin and use cocaine instead, but they do not know how to avoid or deal with overdose. They also know they should stop using drugs but they do not talk openly about it even though many of them have the inner desire to stop."

"It is crucial they open the discussion among themselves," I said, "and talk candidly with each other without hesitation or fear, and support each other to quit. As a group, they can motivate and convince each other to kick the habit better than anyone else on the outside, just as they helped each other to start using drugs."

Tracy started with a prescription pain killer for a toothache. "I was in my teens when my wisdom teeth were removed. I first used Vicodin, then Percocet, and then I started smoking pot just because I wanted to see how it made me feel."

She explained that she had followed her mother into heroin addiction. "My mother shared a needle with me when I was very young. I know she was not thinking straight. I was 16 at the time and I was trying to convince her to stop, but then she let me try. I have been doing it most of my life."

Like Tracy, Lea also started shooting with her mother. "When I was very young, I lost my younger sisters in a house fire. Maybe that was the trigger for my mother's addiction. I don't really know how she started. A couple of years later, both my father and brother died in a car accident. The pain was terrible and everyone who was left in the family was depressed. At that time, Oxycontin was available. Then when my daughter was in her teens, we partied together and smoked all kinds of weed. I knew what I was doing was wrong but I could not stop. I guess I was ashamed and could not figure out how to live normally. I had to face the shame and the fear, but that was too much for me at the time."

She paused, remembering her past. "I lied constantly.

I was obsessed by my need to get high and to search for drugs. I never thought of the consequences and never thought how I was led to commit crimes by my addiction. None of that crosses your mind when your desire to get high is strong. I was totally unaware of what was around me and totally uninhibited. Now I have grandchildren and I tell them not to be ashamed, but rather be content with who they are, regardless how imperfect they see themselves. I tell them not to try to be like anyone else and to learn to say no to their friends and even to their parents when their parents are using drugs. I tell them to believe that they can make a good difference in their parents' lives too."

6. Faith?

Here is my conversation with Victor, a healthy 20-year-old man who was accepted into engineering school but dropped out after his second semester.

"I used drugs and could not study," he said, simply.

"What led you to use drugs? Was school hard for you?"

"School was not hard," he said. He paused for a few moments, then added, "I think I felt a void inside me. In school they teach us about evolution. I became an atheist. I lost meaning for life. I felt my life was going nowhere and I felt helpless in an evil world. I was scared and I stopped caring. I knew who sold drugs and I went to them for something to do. Everywhere there are people with drugs wanting to make a buck."

"But you didn't ask anyone for help—a teacher, a school counselor, your mom, your dad to discuss how you felt?"

"No, it was easier taking drugs than asking for help. My family was dysfunctional, my dad was doing drugs and my mom couldn't fix me."

"You didn't try."

"No, but I knew her fix would be a pep talk. Finding God was what helped me. I don't feel as empty now."

I met Dolla and Sonya at another rehab center. Sonya had been sober for 15 years.

The three of us went to breakfast one day. Over eggs and toast, we discussed the recent presidential races.

Dolla then started, "At one point in my life, I began questioning my existence, the meaning of life, the presence of God and what happens after death. There was a period where I thought my life had no meaning. I was in despair, really depressed. There was nothing to hold on to. I felt if I did good or bad, the outcome of my life was going to be the same. Using drugs was the same as not using drugs—I became indifferent. I felt if I disappeared and died, the world would continue to go on. I even wished I'd die. I did not believe there was a reason to fight. I gave up completely and I started using drugs. It was the only thing that made me feel good at that time."

Sonya agreed. "It is painful to walk through life aimlessly, especially when you are trying to figure out who you are and what you want in life. I remind myself to look around very carefully, to listen to the voices of nature, to write down what I see and hear. When I decided to sober up, I wrote a plan that began with a thank you. Then I wrote down ideas that would get me out of my desire to drink and followed them: I planted a plum tree and a rose bush. I watered them, and walked around the wild flowers, took pictures of nature and chased butterflies. I went to the park and watched sunsets, walked my dog and read a novel. Now I tell others in the same situation to speak with a sober adult or a counselor from school. If no one is available, I say pick up a book and start reading. Pick up a pen and start writing or drawing. Listen to music. Clean your room. Cook for someone. Walk outside. Climb a tree. Turn the radio on, dance, sing, scream, watch TV. Go to the store. Go to the library. It doesn't have to cost money. I learned that when you do something good, you feel good too, no matter how small your deed is. It will propel you to do more of the same and when the next urge to use drugs comes around again, it will be easier to ignore. If you succeed once, you succeed again and again until you have mastered getting away from drugs."

"Destiny is the ultimate mystery to all people. Those who walk towards it with passion in their heart and excitement for what they might discover along the journey are better at dealing with the difficulties of life and they know to live in peace."

"I guess those who have faith are happier than those who don't," Dolla mused. "Faith reveals a sense of hope. I don't necessarily mean religion, although that works for some. I mean faith that everything will work out okay. I had lost hope. I was propelled into obsessive thoughts of fear, pain, depression and anger. I hated myself. But dark moments, like everything else, pass. It's important to believe in something that is powerful and hopeful."

I asked Joanne to imagine it was 10 years ago and to write down her feelings. This is what she wrote: "When I am in pain, I want to escape it. My body and my brain urge me to leave by any means necessary. So I turn to drugs because it's easy. I wish I never started. I always believed I could make it through. Now I have a big banner in my room that lists all the things I can do instead of turning to drugs."

The crime rate increases around people who interact with illegal drugs. When you hurt yourself, you hurt the people around you—whether or not you intend to do so. No one starts with a criminal intention in mind. They are innocent in the beginning, chasing their addiction. But once they turn to drugs, there is no telling how they will behave. Soon, they lose control of a rational mind and enter a new world dominated and ruled by the chemicals in their bodies.

Dolla confessed that her dad killed someone while under the influence of heroin. She recalled him telling her: "There was no excuse for what I did. No one forced me to do any of this. I lost my mind, I lost my temper, but I did not want to kill anyone. You are responsible for what you do, kiddo. You have to use your mind and think, do not turn out like me."

Frank felt more comfortable writing to me instead of

talking face-to-face. He wrote: "I realized that people of all backgrounds can be controlled by drugs. Rich, poor, black and white, living in project housing or in million-dollar homes, it does not matter. All kinds of people were in rehab with me. Everyone struggles. Suffering is inevitable. It is one of the four noble truths of Buddhism. The only way I get through it is with faith. Faith gives me hope, freedom, joy, wholeness—it gives me a purpose. That's all I needed to get out of my addiction."

Frank became a rehab counselor teaching people to have faith and hope. He said, "I can't offer any kind of strength to anyone without hope. We, as humans, can only offer a temporary fix to our problems, and the people I work with have chosen drugs. My goal is to redirect them away from drugs and towards faith and hope."

7. Parents know

Erin is one of seven siblings who grew up in a dysfunctional home. Her father was in the military and rarely around, leaving her mother constantly overwhelmed raising the children by herself. This situation was a source of anger and frustration for the children. Erin did not feel comfortable at home or understood by her mother. She became a dancer at a bar and tried every kind of illegal substance that was available to her.

She told me, "I was never close to my mom; she was abusive. I felt that she always turned her anger on me."

"Did you speak with a teacher?"

"No, I wasn't a good student. The atmosphere stressed me out and I couldn't study. I just figured that my teacher would tell me to focus on my school work and be a good student."

"What drugs did you take?"

"I started with meth and cocaine."

"When you look back now, do you think you should have told your mom how you felt?"

"Yes. Now that I am a parent, I know that my mom was stressed and she took it out on me. At the time, I didn't think she cared about me or she knew what to do to help me. As a parent now, I know that if I had spoken to her, she probably would have realized how her behavior affected me and my siblings. She could have tried to help me even though she was stressed."

"Did you take steps to hide your drugs?" I asked.

"Yes. And at one time I was dealing, so I would find the most inconspicuous places I could think of. I hid them inside the caps of my lipstick and pens. I taped them under my bed, stuffed them in dirty socks and empty soda cans, inside air vents, inside my books and my sheets. I kept my room messy on purpose and I dug holes in dry walls and covered them with pictures. One of my favorite places was in the attic behind the insulation and inside old dusty boxes."

Children sometimes think their parents are ignorant and they don't care about them. They prefer to deal with their issues by themselves rather than talk to their parents. Sometimes parents do not have the appropriate answers because of the complexity of the situation. Addiction often leads to mental health issues as a result of an imbalance in the brain caused by the chemicals used, and these two factors require high expertise most people do not have. It is a long process to diagnose a mental illness, to diagnose addiction, or to complete a successful rehab. It also takes the willingness of the person affected to make a change.

"But sober parents will know how to guide you even when it appears that there is no solution in sight," said Erin, who has been drug-free for 15 years. "Sometimes we interpret our own feelings and perceptions instead of what our parents are saying. Anger and frustration often overshadow what they really mean to say and how much love they have in their heart for their children."

Kim told me that she used drugs only once. "I was mad at my parents. They argued constantly and I grew tired of it. I went to a friend's house one evening and she had a few people over shooting heroin. It was a weak moment and I did what they did."

"Once?"

"Yes. My mother went looking for me. She appeared weak to me, but she was strong and had talked to me about not doing drugs. I knew I needed to stop no matter what. She made it clear that I needed to make new friends, so I did. I stayed away."

8. "College is Where You Drink"

Kyle was completing his graduate studies when we initially met. He brought his younger brother, Mark to our meeting. Kyle used to believe that the world around him was very competitive, selfish and cruel.

"The higher you want to go in your career, the more competition there is," he told me. "It tired me to think about the future. Even though I went to graduate school, I was not sure I would find a job. And I did not for a while, so I turned to drugs." He paused then added, "initially, I wanted to experiment. I had time on my hands."

After a few moments Mark added, "College is where you drink. You can easily find lots of people like yourself doing the things you want to do in college. Education does not prevent this from happening. On the contrary, the highest amounts of drinking happen in college among educated students. You want to fit in, so you do what others are doing. My friends and I only focused on smoking pot and doing drugs; we did not care about socializing with others. We stayed away from people who didn't use drugs."

"These behaviors have caused many deaths," I said.

"Yes. But college is supposed to be fun. No one is thinking of death in college. We used cocaine but we stayed away from heroin because it is addicting. It was fun at the time."

"How did it affect your life?"

"Poorly. I didn't focus on my studies and got below-average grades, which affected my job prospects. That left me with a bad attitude, which caused relationship problems with my parents and siblings."

"If you could do it over and go to college now, what would you do?"

"Even though I know what I should have done, I am

not sure I could have done it differently back then. Had I known, I may have acted differently. But I didn't know."

"What would you tell your children now to prevent them from falling into the same situation you were in?"

"I would open a frank discussion with them. I would keep them busy with school activities, camps, anything to occupy their time. I would make sure they studied to get good grades and I would play with them. Parents should know their kids so they can detect changes in their behavior. Those early signs can save lives.

"Teenagers like to take chances in life, they like to experiment and try new things. This is normal at their age and it is important to discovering themselves. But some changes are unsafe. They get tattoos, dye their hair, and pierce their body, and they also take drugs and drink. It will be important for them to know what they are getting themselves into, in order to make the proper decision before they start using drugs and alcohol."

9. The Star Inside

Most people we spoke with had a common goal in life. They want to have a family, play with their children, earn a decent living and do good in society. But the drugs took hold of them before their dreams came true.

People who turn to drugs are typically very sensitive and they see and feel problems afflicting their life and society, sometimes more acutely than other people. They may have the ability to contribute solutions to these societal problems, but often they don't speak up. Instead, they use drugs to escape their unhappiness and frustrations. They do not see their own star inside. But if they were to look for it and discover it, their behavior would change and they would increase the odds of attaining their goals in life.

Problems can't be solved if they are not acknowledged. It is the beginning of a solution to figure out what the problems are. We want you to have the confidence to reveal your concerns and your problems. Together, we can work on a solution before you start using drugs. Because at that point, it may be too late.

10. Rebellion

In the neighborhood where Joe grew up, alcohol and drugs were very prevalent.

"Did you feel pressured to join the other kids?"

"No, no one pressured me. I grew up with those kids. They were like brothers and sisters. I wanted to be like them so I did what they did. I did not ask but they offered. At that time, none of them seemed to have a problem, so I didn't think I would have a problem either."

"Where did you get the money to pay for it?"

"My friend stole a case of liquor and we sold it to buy crack cocaine."

"Then what happened?"

"It felt good, so I wanted more. I had no money, so I started selling crack to support my own habit, but ended up on crack myself."

"Were you ever caught?"

"Yes. I went to jail many times. I am very regretful."

"What advice do you have for others?"

"Don't ever, ever, ever start. That's what I tell my grandkids all the time. I took them to my old neighborhood where drug use is still common. I showed them what they would look like if they ended up living on the streets."

After years of rehab, Joe became a drug counselor.

"The number of kids and young people using illegal drugs is growing and it breaks my heart," he said. "We have not solved the problem. We don't get involved until after they have committed crimes and then we call them criminals and we throw them in jail. That won't fix the problem. Their self esteem drops because now they are criminals. Once they take the wrong path, going back to a normal life becomes nearly impossible. They miss out.

It's a snowball effect. Once you miss a few days of life, it becomes easier and easier to give up on life altogether. And how do you catch up? Personally, I don't know if I ever caught up with all the years I lost."

After a short pause, he continued: "Once you are addicted to drugs, you'll feel like a failure. It has happened to every person I counsel. You've disappointed yourself, your parents, and your family. You really need help because it will take a long time to remove these negative thoughts and feelings and bring joy and self-esteem back into your life."

Anthony has always been quiet. He felt he would sound dumb asking questions he should know the answers to.

"Withholding your questions is ultimately withholding your own knowledge," I told him. "It is blocking your creativity."

"We were poor; we had nothing," he told me of his life growing up during the 1970s recession. "If we had money, it would have been different for me. My dad lost everything in the stock market. Lots of people made money when dad was losing. I wanted to escape what was happening."

"You escaped but you hurt yourself in the process."

"I had no intention of hurting myself. Everything started as harmless fun. You're drinking beer at a party, with no idea you'll become a drunk. No one sits on their porch and says, 'I want to become a heroin addict.'"

"Did you ever think of your parents' feelings?"

"I had two working parents who hardly spent time with us. They always told us to go to school and be good. They never said anything else."

"What did they say when you went to jail?"

"I broke their heart ....three times. I went to rehab, but it did no good. This country needs more funding for drug rehab. The waiting lists are so long and if you're not intoxicated when you show up for rehab, they put you at the end of the list. When you're on the waiting list, you have nowhere to go except back to the street. So you go back to the same people and you end up using drugs again and again. Rehab centers need enough money to take everyone who needs help. Then they need to help them find jobs."

Jane struck me as an intelligent woman. As I spoke to her, I found myself surprised to learn that she had been a heroin user.

"I left home at 18 to follow my partner, but she dumped me. I went to visit a friend who had a drug stash."

"Why not go back to your family?"

"I never met my dad and I did not have a good relationship with my mother. She did not approve of my relationship with a woman, so I rebelled and I was too proud to go back."

11. "Dropping Dead Like Flies"

On a train to New York City, I met Piper. She was afflicted with serious psychological problems and post-traumatic stress disorder from seeing her friends dying in front of her. She explained: "I spent a lot of time with people who would get together and shoot up different drugs. We always thought we could quit when we wanted to."

"Can you tell me what you went through?"

"I saw people dropping dead like flies. They were all younger than 25. Even though I survived, the memory of their death still haunts me. I'll never forget how they were lying motionless on the floor, two or three of them at one time, and the rest of us helplessly not knowing what to do. This pain will never leave me; it ruined my psyche until this day."

"Did their deaths change your behavior?"

"Not in that moment. I didn't have time to think because I had several overdoses myself."

"Did they call for help when you overdosed?"

"Oh no. No one ever asked for help or offered any. We never called 911. When someone overdosed, we poured cold water on them and hoped they would make it."

"What drugs did you use?"

"We used to call them Ts and Bs. Now people use more dangerous products that are mixed with who knows what. That is why more are dying nowadays than ever before."

"Can you describe how drugs made you feel?"

"I enjoyed it a lot the first time, but after that initial time, you are always chasing that first feeling. You will never get that first feeling back, and you use higher and higher doses but you are never satisfied like the first time. That's how people get hooked."

"Did you go to rehab?"

"No. You have to decide by yourself to stay away from the people who do this kind of stuff." She paused. "But I am still in therapy. You can't ever wipe these memories from your head. There is no treatment for that. I deeply regret ever starting."

Emma lost her son when he was 22. JP was using heroin with his friends and collapsed in front of them. Instead of calling for help, his friends walked to Emma's house to tell her that something was wrong with JP.

"I am angry. I am sad. Day or night, I feel like I am trapped in a twister that will never release me."

She lifts her arms up and grabs her head. "I can't rest. What hurts me the most is that JP's friends did not call 911. Had they done that, JP may have been saved.

Not only is his life gone; my life is over also. The only thing left in me is pain."

Only their stories live.
Maybe now the lonely souls, broken hearts and ailing
bodies can read and grasp on to these stories,
and begin to heal.

A unique look at drug and alcohol abuse and prevention. By incorporating first-person accounts of addiction survivors, a doctor shares her perspective on the risks of substance abuse.

Jamilé Wakim Fleming is board-certified in diseases of the liver and the gastrointestinal system. She has published several manuscripts and chapter books in her field of expertise and has focused her career on the prevention and treatment of illnesses that affect the liver. Her passion is to prevent teens from using any form of addicting substance.

Oriana Marie is an English major at Loyola University. She has provided invaluable insight into substance abuse problems facing high school and college students.

Donna M. Lauer was a research analyst for a federal agency for more than 20 years and has conducted extensive research into drug trends on a national, state and local level.

Cover illustration by Jawad Wakim.